THE CONCISE HISTORIES OF **DEVON**

GEORGIAN DEVON

THE CONCISE HISTORIES OF **DEVON**

THE
MINT
PRESS

GEORGIAN
DEVON

JEREMY BLACK

First published in Great Britain by The Mint Press, 2003

ISBN 1-903356-28-8

Cataloguing in Publication Data
CIP record for this title is available from the British Library

The Mint Press
18 The Mint
Exeter, Devon
England EX4 3BL

Cover and text design by Delphine Jones

Main cover illustration: Bust of Thomas Vivian, early eighteenth century (by courtesy of Exeter Museum Service)

Coin: George II tuppence (by courtesy of Exeter Museums Service.)

Printed and bound in Great Britain
by Short Run Press Ltd, Exeter.

CONTENTS

For Richard Hitchcock, a much
valued colleague

The closer we are to the past, the more misleading it can be. The Georgian Age (1714-1830) seems so close thanks to television and film treatments of novels by Henry Fielding and Jane Austen. To help us identify with characters such as Tom Jones and Emma, they are made to seem like us. Go to Saltram and you will see where Austen's Sense and Sensibility was filmed. And if we turn to the scholarship, the stress is often on how the period was becoming like the modern or even today. Superstition was banished and there was a `big bang' made up of the `Age of Reason', the Industrial Revolution, the rise of the `public sphere' – newspapers and coffee houses to you and me, and of democratic aspirations, and, also, a series of changes, including better communications (canals, turnpikes and postal services) that speeded up life and led to the spread of the new.

As with most dominant interpretations, there is much that is true about this portrayal, and, insofar as it affects Devon, it will be discussed in this book. Yet, it is far less than a complete account and one of my tasks is to offer a different, less `progressive', view of Devon under the first four Georges.

Aside from asking you to suspend your faith in the usual view, I also want you to consider an age in which Devon was considerably more important than it is now. Before the rise of coal-based industry, the north of England, the West Midlands, the central belt of Scotland, and South Wales were all less important (and in relative terms less populous) than they were to become. Instead, it was the south of England that was important not only because it was the most fertile agricultural region, but also because much industry was still located there.

Devon was important on both counts, especially the latter, at the start of our period. It also had a rich maritime legacy, with both fishing and trade important activities. Aside from providing value to the county, Devon's maritime role was also important to the country and to the British Atlantic. Lastly, as the seat of numerous MPs, Devon was not without political importance, although the politics of Britain were local and national rather than county in character.

THE
COUNTY

Think not of Devon today, a county of a million people with large urban areas and a road system that can take you from one side to the other in less than half a day. Think, instead, of Devon in 1714, a largely rural county where distance kept most people for most of the time in their own neighbourhoods, where travel, particularly by land, was difficult and where the dark, the damp and the cold pressed hard on people. Think of a Devon where injury and illness that we now regard as posing few problems, instead were killers.

Hardship and anxiety exaggerated the impact of distance. So did topography. Devon was not like much of southern England. Although parts of East Devon, the Exe valley and the South Hams were fertile and relatively well-drained, much of the county was far less welcome to the traveller or the farmer, than, say, Wiltshire or Dorset. The combination of all or some of heavy rainfall, poor soils, rocky terrain and high land with the reduction in growing season that that brought was a particular problem. They helped ensure that much of the county was difficult arable land and more suited for animal husbandry. However, the limited nature of communication links ensured that there was a greater need for all-round agricultural production than was to be the case by the late nineteenth century, and, still more, today. The detailed pattern of land-use was far more complex than might be suggested by upland pasture and lowland arable. In upland areas grain was grown in small quantities as a subsistence crop. This accentuated the difficult nature of agriculture and has left evidence in the form of signs of one-time cultivation in moorland Devon. Livestock were kept in lowland areas to provide meat, milk, manure, wool and motive power.

At the level of the individual farmstead, and again of the village, there was a degree of self-reliance that is totally alien to modern farmers. This reflected the relative difficulty of preservation and transport in an age before refrigeration and motor vehicles, but also the degree and intensity of local systems of exchange, as well as the degree to which self- and local-reliance made more economic sense than in the modern age of specialisation through comparative profit margins.

TRANSPORT

Communication problems helped 'shape' the county very differently to today. Valleys were prone to flood and their soil was often heavy and difficult to traverse. Instead, most land routes sought to follow ridges where the soil was drier, and bridging points, such as Exeter, took a central role in the communication system. So also did ferries. There was no road crossing of the Tamar downriver of Gunnislake until the Tamar Bridge at

Saltash was opened in 1961. This helped ensure that the divide between Cornwall and Devon was far greater than was to be the case once a rail link had been constructed.

The difficulties of land transport, not least the draft animals required to pull laden wagons, led to an emphasis on water transport. In Devon, this meant the sea. There was no major waterway system equivalent to that of the Trent.

This emphasis on the sea helped to divide the county. The towns of North Devon, Barnstaple, Bideford and Ilfracombe (the harbour of which was enlarged in 1760 and 1824-9), were important because they were ports. As such they looked not across the land to Tiverton, Exeter or Plymouth but across the sea to South Wales, southern Ireland or, more particularly, Bristol, which dominated the economy of the Bristol Channel.

Similarly, the coastal towns of South Devon were linked by the water to each other and further afield. Not that sea travel was easy. Storms claimed many lives. In addition, there were too few lighthouses or other helps to navigators. In the Bristol Channel, Lundy's reefs claimed many ships and the construction of the Old Light on Lundy, a major lighthouse completed in 1820, was long overdue.

By 1830 the transport system had changed greatly and Devon as a county had more meaning therefore as an economic and social unit. Roads, not canals, were the key to developments in the South West. After the failure of the short canal opened near St Austell in Cornwall in about 1720, none was opened in the region until the Stover Canal in

1794, which was designed to carry pottery clay; although there was interest in new links in the intervening period. This reflected an openness to profitable changes. Beavis Woods, Town Clerk of Tiverton, recorded on 24 October 1768:

> *A subscription is set on foot here to raise a sum of money to bring down Mr [James] Brindley to take a survey of the country in order to make a navigable canal through part of Somerset and down by way of Taunton and Tiverton or Cullompton to Exeter or Topsham. Subscriptions have also been opened for this purpose at Exeter, Cullompton, Uffculme and other parts of this neighbourhood... people in general (gentlemen and others) seem in earnest and I believe such a scheme very practicable and advantageous.*

In practice of the planned Grand Western Canal from Taunton to Topsham (for which a Parliamentary Act was passed in 1796) the section from Tiverton to the Somerset border was completed and opened in 1814, but, thereafter, only the section from there to Taunton was built. The opening of the Bristol and Exeter railway in 1844 superseded this canal route.

Other canals in the county included the Tavistock Canal in 1817 between the town and Morwellham Quay on the Tamar, which included a tunnel nearly a mile and a half long; a branch to Millhill Quarries opened in 1819; a canal from Great Torrington to near Bideford opened in 1827; and the Bude Canal opened in 1823 and 1825, which opened up links with Devon but did not reach Holsworthy as intended: the canal had been intended to bring sand inland in order to improve the hill soils. More successfully, although an attempt to extend it to Crediton had failed in 1810, the Exeter Canal was lengthened (and its banks raised) in 1825 to 1827, enabling ships of up to 400 tons to sail up to Exeter where a basin was opened in 1830. However, the county's canals did not join to form part of a regional or national system.

Roads made more of a difference in Devon. The first turnpike trust in the county, the Exeter Trust, was established in 1753, and was rapidly followed by many others, leading to major improvements. Turnpike trusts were bodies authorised by Parliament to raise capital in order to repair and build roads and to charge travellers to these ends. There were twenty turnpike trusts in the county by

1772, and by 1800 there were turnpikes across much of the county, including one across Dartmoor, although there was none between Bideford and Launceston, while the South Hams was poorly served and there was none from Ilfracombe to Lynton. The new roads were the routes followed by coach services carrying both passengers and freight. They speeded the movement of letters and newspapers. All contributed to a potent sense of change.

Alongside lists that suggest steady improvement, it is important to note episodes that lead towards a less optimistic conclusion. Thus the group of bridges over the watercourses of the River Otter at Fenny Bridges on the major route east of Exeter were reported as in a poor state of repair to the Quarter Sessions in 1704. The parishioners of Gittisham were able to show that the parish was too poor to carry out the necessary repairs, and, when the sessions provided fifteen pounds, requests from other parishes for their bridges led the court to rescind the money. A report was ordered, but none was made until 1711 when the court was told that a local landowner, Lady Kirkham, had conveyed nearby land on trust to provide funds for bridge repairs. However, the trustees declared that the profits from the land were insufficient and claimed to be responsible for the bridges in Feniton parish and not in Gittisham, an interpretation that was challenged. The court took the charity into its hands, but it was not until 1723 that the trustees provided the accounts ordered in 1714. Deciding that they had money in hand that should have been used for bridge repairs, the magistrates ordered the trustees to pay it into court, but the trustees refused and the administration of the trust was not settled by the High Court of Chancery until 1750, the year in which Dr Richard Pococke recorded being delayed several hours by the river flooding. A new brick arch bridge was built at Fenny in 1769, but it had to be rebuilt in 1809 after complaints in 1797 and an indictment of the county in 1806 for not keeping the bridge in repair. North Devon was another area with difficulties. In 1787 the coach journey from Exeter to Barnstaple took over twelve hours.

Despite such problems, there were important improvements. For example, in 1774 the opening of the Countess Wear Bridge provided a bridging point over the Exe below Exeter. Improvements continued in the early nineteenth century. A series of often quite small-scale changes greatly improved the system. For example, the Honiton and Ilminster Turnpike Trust constructed a new road from Yarde to near Ilminster from 1807 to 1812 and the Cullompton Turnpike Trust constructed another from near Broadclyst to near Cullompton from 1813 to 1816.

There was also a process of improvement to existing routes. In the 1820s and early 1830s, the worst routes of the Exeter Turnpike Trust were replaced. This led to smoother and more level roads and therefore to an ability to pull heavy loads. The widening of Devon roads in the 1820s also helped the replacement of packhorses by wheeled traffic. The use of macadam, for example, on the Exeter to Exmouth turnpike in 1819, greatly helped with durability.

There were important improvements before the steam railway reached Devon.

Non-suspension bridges were opened over the estuaries of the Teign and the Plym in 1827, opening up much of South Devon to road traffic; the former, Shaldon Bridge, was then the longest in Britain. Steam and chain floating bridges followed at Dartmouth, Saltash and Torpoint. Such improvements helped to cut journey times, and therefore travel costs, and to integrate Devon into the national economy. R. K. Newman, an Exeter MP of the 1820s, told a House of Commons Select Committee that `since the roads have been improved... a very large amount of the produce of the country is daily sent from Devon to the Metropolis [London]'. These new roads became the routes for expanding coach and wagon services. By 1828, coaches were running four times a day between Exeter and both Exmouth and

Teignmouth, while journey times to London and other centres had been greatly cut.

THE
ECONOMY

Although Devon played its role in the communications revolution, the same was less true of agriculture and industry. There was improvement in both spheres. However, the organisational possibilities, centred on enclosure, that were so important across much of the country in the eighteenth century, were less so in Devon, because, by 1500, much of it had already been enclosed. As a result, there was not the sweeping change seen, in particular, in the Midlands. There were however, developments, for example, by 1750 the use of lime to help counteract soil acidity, was virtually universal among the better Devon farmers. Across much of the county, the combination of poor soils, steep slopes, a limited growing season and high relief encouraged dependence on animal rearing. In steep areas this meant sheep; on flatter (and lower) land, cattle. Neither, especially sheep-rearing, offered a form of agriculture that could support the population levels of arable regions, or encouraged their nucleated (village) settlements. Instead, dispersed settlement was the norm, frequently in the form of isolated farmsteads. There were also important advances in cattle breeding in the late eighteenth and early nineteenth centuries. These led to an improvement in meat yields and to Devon acquiring a strong reputation in the field, with Devon cattle prized by London butchers while farmers sought to improve their herds.

The success of animal husbandry contributed greatly to the county's agricultural prosperity, but, in relative terms, it suffered from the developments elsewhere in England during the eighteenth century, especially the spread of root crops as a means to maintain soil fertility in East Anglia and the impact of enclosure. Furthermore, there were other important limits on agricultural improvement. Price movements did not reward the improvers until after 1760. Many farms were too small and the legacy of established practice pressed hard. It was not easily possible to alter the size, shape or nature of fields, nor the farm buildings and yards. Most small farmers lacked the necessary capital and willingness to accept risk for a programme of improvement. In the section of his *General Survey, from personal experience, observation, and enquiry, of the Rural Economy of England* dealing with Devon, which was published in 1796, the farmer and agricultural writer William Marshall described West Devon as the most unimpressive part of the country. Illiteracy also limited receptiveness to agricultural innovations.

The attitude of landowners to agricultural reform varied greatly. The availability of capital was an important issue. John Parker, 1st Earl of Morley, the owner of the Saltram estate, in 1806-7 drained the wet lands to the south-west of the house by constructing an embankment along the Plym estuary, reclaiming 175 acres, thenceforth known as Chelson Meadow. The cost is reported to have been over £15,000. Such expenditure was beyond the reach of most landowners and indeed, Parker had to mortgage the estate. His approach was a mix of the dominant `improvement' attitude of the age and a dangerous profligacy. Under the former head, Parker also built a dock at Turnchapel in 1800, while in 1825-7 he built a new bridge across the Laira, at a cost of £30,000. Parker died leaving liabilities of £258,000.

Rising demand for food benefited landlords and tenant farmers, not the landless poor. Agricultural wages remained below fifteenth-century levels in real terms. Social tensions in rural areas can be seen with poaching. The Game Laws were widely regarded as unfair, while the gentry viewed challenges to them as theft and as threats to the preservation of the social order. From the late eighteenth century, game preserves came to be protected by spring guns and mantraps.

With industry, again, it is necessary to distinguish between the situation in Devon, which was relatively satisfactory, and the relative position of Devon's industries, which was less welcome. For example, the marked growth of textile production in Lancashire and Yorkshire was, in part, achieved at the expense of traditional centres of production, such as Exeter, Colchester and Worcester. Labour was cheaper in Lancashire and Yorkshire and the textile industry less restricted by corporation traditions. However, some Devon industries remained active. The export of serges, a type of cloth popular on the continent, as well as in Britain, from Exeter, the leading fulling and finishing centre in the West Country, rose from 120,000 pieces in the 1680s to 365,000 in

1710, a quarter of England's entire cloth exports, before falling to 162,802 in 1745. Thereafter, thanks to demand from the East India Company, exports revived to peak at 390,000 in 1777, although British and European markets had been largely taken by East Anglia and Yorkshire competition. By 1800, only 8,126 pieces were exported from Exeter.

Devon's relative industrial position deteriorated as part of a general crisis of industry in southern England from the late eighteenth century, as coal-based manufacturing, factories and other factors encouraged development elsewhere. For example, from the 1780s, the woollen textile industry of the West Riding of Yorkshire acquired a price advantage over competitors such as those in Devon.

The importance of new technology and entrepreneurial energy was demonstrated at Tiverton where John Heathcoat founded a machine-made net and lace factory. The threat to jobs posed by his patented bobbin net machines had led to the riotous destruction of his Loughborough factory in 1816, and Heathcoat moved his machines to a disused Tiverton cotton mill, built in 1792. This factory hit lace-making in East Devon (where it was prominent in Honiton and Ottery St Mary), but also showed what could be achieved in the absence of coal. A former partner of Heathcoat, John Boden, opened the Derby Lace Works to the east of Barnstaple in 1825. By 1830, he was employing 1,000 people and, largely as a result, the population of the town rose from 5,079 in 1821 to 7,902 in 1841. The lifestyle and densely–inhabited working-class neighbourhood that developed there and in Tiverton were relatively uncommon in the county.

Agricultural processing provided many opportunities across the South West. This was true for leather production and related industries, for example glove-making, and also for paper-making. Cider production was also very important. Nevertheless, while these industries provided jobs, they did not offer the profits gained from processing products from outside Europe, principally cotton, sugar-cane and tobacco, none of which became notable in Devon, nor the growth to be gained from coal-based mechanization. There is scant information about Devon mining for most of the eighteenth century but, by the close of the century, there was much tin mining on Dartmoor, copper mining in the nearby Tamar valley and one of Europe's leading supplies of manganese near Newton St Cyres and Upton Pyne. Copper mining developed and became more profitable in the 1820s, thanks in part to new investment.

However, the mining that was the base of industry elsewhere did not develop. The iron mines that were established, particularly in North Molton and the Brendon Hills, were small scale and there was no coal. The last was fundamental to the level of Devon's economic activity. A major coalfield in Dartmoor might have turned Plymouth into a city with an economic base comparable to Cardiff, Glasgow or Newcastle, while Exeter would have been like Chester or Durham, a testimony to older, different values, close to a major economic zone.

SOCIETY

A lack of industrial growth in Devon affected employment prospects for a population that, as elsewhere in the country, rapidly grew from the mid-eighteenth century. Due to poverty, the poor, both rural and urban, were very exposed to changes in the price of food and generally lived in inadequate housing. As they could not afford much fuel, the poor were often cold and wet in the winter and were more commonly in the dark. The circumstances of their life made them prone to disease, although disease was also a social leveller. Malnutrition stunted growth, hit energy levels and reduced resistance to ill-health. Poor diet encouraged colon parasitic infection, hepatitis and salmonella.

It is necessary to be wary of finding signs of modernity in the social and domestic life of the period. It is all too easy to assume that life was in many respects similar to ours. There are few signs for the superficial viewer of more profound contrasts, contrasts that assure us that the very experience of life was totally different. The demographics were chilling. Individual and collective experiences were affected by the age of the individual observer. The average experience of life for the people of the period came at a younger age than for their descendants today, and was shaped within a context of the ever-present threat of death, disease, injury and pain.

Alongside long-lasting individuals, there were lives quickly cut short, in the case of women especially in childbirth. Sir Hugh Acland (1637-1713), the owner of Killerton, survived his son John and was succeeded by his grandson, another Hugh, who lived from only 1696 until 1728. Of the Parkers of Saltram, four of the five who headed the family between 1649 and 1840 had two wives. Several of these wives died young; after Frances, first wife of John Parker, 1st Lord Boringdon (1734-88), died in 1764, he married Theresa (1744-75), but she died soon after the birth of her second child, another Theresa. Other [sic], 3rd Earl of Plymouth, married Elizabeth Lewis in 1730, only for him to die aged twenty-five, his wife to follow a year later, and the estates to be inherited by the 4th Earl, at the age of eighteen months, under the guardianship of his grandfather. The 4th Earl died in 1771 and his son, the 5th Earl (1751-99), who was described as `a fine fat round English Lord loves eat', was by 1794 `in a very bad way, for he is very near blind, and his legs are so swelled that it is thought he is going into a dropsy'. His son and heir had an even shorter life (1789-1833).

These were wealthy individuals with some chance of quality living. The situation for the `lower orders' was bleaker on average. It has been suggested that the county's population grew from 227,157 in 1660 to 358,987 in 1805, with the urban rate of increase being greater than that in the countryside. Population growth was concentrated in the period from the mid

1740s on, with life expectancy at birth in England rising from an average lifespan of about 30 for those born in the 1680s to 42 by the 1750s. In addition, marital fertility among women aged thirty-five and over rose from mid-century. This was probably the consequence of a fall in stillbirths and can be seen as evidence of rising average living standards. There were some improvements in health care, not least the use of inoculation against smallpox, while the Devon and Exeter Hospital opened in 1743; but defences against disease remained flimsy. The exposed state of the population was captured in an item in the *Salisbury and Winchester Journal* of 25 October 1790:

> *Last week died in a state of canine madness Miss Tomkins near Exeter. What is very remarkable this young lady had never been bit, but received her death, it is thought, by permitting*

*a dog to run about the house after
being bit by a mad dog. This should
be a caution to many unthinking
people, who suffer such dogs to run
about the house, never considering
that the poison remains on the coat of
the animal and by this means is
communicated to their clothes, etc.*

Another form of vulnerability was that
to fire. Wood and thatch burned readily and
fire fighting faced many limitations. Devon
homes suffered accordingly. Tiverton, for
example, was hit hard in 1726, 1730 and,
especially 1731, the last leading to an Act
that all roofs thereafter should be of lead,
slate or tile. Crediton lost 460 houses to a
savage fire in 1743. Much of Honiton was
rebuilt after fires in 1747 and 1765.

As far as the poor were concerned,
there was scant understanding of the
problems posed by unemployment and

under-employment, and such hardships were treated as self-inflicted and thus deserving of neglect or punishment. The standard precept of care was that it should discriminate between the deserving and the undeserving. This religio-moral principle was applied on grounds of age, health and gender, not with reference to employment or income. Thus, the infirm, the elderly, the young, and women with children were the prime beneficiaries of poor relief, while the able-bodied, whether in low-paid employment or unemployed, were denied it.

The financial and administrative system organised in the Elizabethan Poor Law, with compulsory poor rates, remained until the 1834 Poor Law Amendment Act. Poor-relief was seen as a considerable burden. In 1787, John Rolle (1756-1842), MP for the county from 1780 until he was created Lord Rolle in 1796, proposed a radical response. `At the express desire of his constituents' and in response to `the very heavy and increasing [poor] rates', Rolle suggested a national fund provided by progressive taxation and compulsory national insurance. Nothing came of this.

Able-bodied men unable to find work were treated as rogues and vagabonds. The Poor Relief Act of 1662 made the right to relief dependent upon the pauper being settled in the parish, a practice that led to the expulsion of paupers deemed non-resident. Individuals could only remain in a new parish if they had a settlement certificate stating that their former parish would support them if they became a burden on the poor rate.

A growing institutionalism of poor relief was seen in the eighteenth century.

It involved specific facilities and also taking forward the provision under the Elizabethan Poor Law Acts that overseers of the poor should try to find them work. Exeter had a workhouse to provide poor relief. However, over the county, too few workhouses were founded to deal with the problems of poverty. Workhouses remained less important than `outdoor relief': providing assistance, and sometimes work, to the poor in their own homes. This had the virtue of flexibility, not least in dealing with the seasonal problems of unemployment, under-employment and dearth that the variations of work in agriculture, industry and transport produced. A seasonal need for relief was best served through outdoor relief rather than through institutionalism. The `Old' (pre-1834) Poor Law is often condemned as ineffective or repressive, but it was an adaptable system offering a satisfactory response to the needs of many communities. As with the political and ecclesiastical institutions and practices of the period, it is important, alongside contemporary criticism and eventual replacement, to note the longevity and general success of the system.

Educational access and provision also reflected social power and assumptions. Because so many children worked, their access to formal education was limited. Attendance at school was lower in summer, the high point of agricultural work, than in winter. Education was not supported by taxation, central or local. Education had to be paid for by the pupil's family, which was generally the case in grammar schools, or by a benefactor, dead or alive. There were many `petty' charity schools, often known as `dame schools'. Some took more children in return for payments. But for every child who acquired some education, there were others who received none. Girls and the rural population had fewer educational opportunities than boys and town-dwellers.

The poor who were educated were offered less. There was a general assumption in charity schools that the pupils should be provided with a vocational education, which meant teaching employable skills, as well as the morality that contributed to good conduct. These requirements were laid out in the terms of the bequests under which charity schools operated. Thus, spinning, weaving, and knitting were taught to girls. Morality was provided by discipline and by the teaching of the fundamentals: the catechism, the creed, the commandments, and the Lord's Prayer. The Classical teaching offered by the grammar schools was not available in most schools, but nor also in many was free mathematics.

TRADE

Devon remained important for shipping. Ships from Dartmouth, Plymouth, and Bideford had dominated the Newfoundland fishery in the 1670s. By the 1770s, the leading ports in the fishery were Dartmouth, Exeter and Poole. Bideford played a role in the tobacco trade, but it could not sustain its role. Although its foreign trade declined in the early and mid-eighteenth century, Plymouth was Devon's leading port. In part, this reflected the need to import naval stores for the naval base. Smuggling was also important.

While Devon's foreign trade grew in the period, it became proportionately less important within Britain as a whole. In part, this reflected the absence of a dynamic coal-based hinterland to match those served by Glasgow and Liverpool, but other factors also played a role. There was nothing to match the re-export trade seen at these ports as well as at Whitehaven, nor a breadth of activity to match Bristol. Compared to Bristol, there was a fall in foreign-going tonnage from the 1750s. The Devon fleet increasingly concentrated on coastal vessels, which lacked the profitability of foreign trade.

The towns in the country grew; `Plymouth' became the most populous, rising to 43,194 inhabitants in 1801, although Plymouth, Stonehouse and Devonport were not joined as a single county borough until 1914. The area's growth reflected development in the dockyards. As a result, the population of Plymouth Dock, renamed Devonport in 1824, had a population larger than that of Plymouth in 1823. Exeter had been the leading town by population in the mid eighteenth century, but, by the start of the nineteenth, that of `Plymouth' was more than twice as large. Tiverton and Barnstaple were the next ranking Devon towns.

WAR
WITH
FRANCE

The emphasis on confronting France, which dominated British military planning for most of the period, led to a stress on the value of Plymouth. Despite efforts in the 1780s to develop a major port at Cherbourg, the French lacked a significant naval base in the Channel. Instead, their major naval bases (other than Toulon on the Mediterranean) were to the west: Brest in particular but also Rochefort. The same was also true of

Cadiz and Ferrol for Spain. These ports were best watched by British warships as far to the west as necessary and thus not needing to make headway against westerlies in order to leave the Channel as was the case for the ships based at Portsmouth and even more, Chatham. As the blockade of Brest (and other ports) became the crucial tool of maritime protection, so it was important to develop naval facilities at Plymouth, and this was accentuated with the development, from 1759, of close blockade. Loose blockade had given the French a chance to put to sea, but close blockade sought to deprive the French of such an opportunity to take the initiative.

Whether loose or close, the presence of a large fleet in the Western Approaches had many consequences for Devon. It provided a ready market for local farmers and businessmen, but that helped drive up the cost of food. In April 1795, the resulting higher prices led to riots. The navy and the dockyard also provided jobs. The dockyard workforce rose from 54 in 1691 to 1,837 in 1759. Initially, in 1689, it was decided that the Plymouth dry dock should be capable of receiving up to third-rates, but in 1691 the dock contracts were upgraded so as to be able to take the biggest ships of the line. This was also linked to the development of fortifications there in order to protect the harbour from attack, a plan that led to a parliamentary controversy in 1786. The eighteenth-century slipways of Devonport Dockyard survive, as do the roperies. In Stonehouse the Naval Hospital, laid out in 1758-62, survives, as does the Victualling Yard built on reclaimed land from 1825 to 1833.

War did lead to a sense of vulnerability. In December 1745, as the French threatened to invade in support of the Jacobites, Stephen Weston, Registrar of the diocese of Exeter, complained:

I doubt not shall any attempt be made from Brest or St Malo at this time we should fall a too easy prey since land forces we have none but the garrison at Plymouth, that just now reduced by a draught for Bristol; part of our Western Squadron too being lately sailed to strengthen [Admiral] Vernon in the Downs [off Kent], I think we are in a state to be pitied, and the utmost to be hoped from us is to run away with the money we are raising, leaving our estates and houses to the rage of the invaders. We must pray therefore for a North East or North West wind to shut up the western ports of France since a South East or South West brings our enemies upon us, and at the same time denies us the assistance of our friends.

Weston also drew attention to the ambiguous local response to the loyal subscription:

The Tories won't help us, and some of the Whigs who love their money better than themselves say this is only taxing the King's best friends. Lord Clinton has refused by telling us its unconstitutional.

Confrontation with France led not only to the improvement of naval facilities but also to the building of barracks, for example in Exeter and, also, as part of the Berry Head fortifications built to the east of Brixham between 1794 and 1804; and to an important militia and volunteer movement. The *British Gazette and Public*

Advertiser of 12 January 1804, reported three days earlier in Devon Volunteer units had staged elaborate manoeuvres:

> *The Exeter Volunteer regiment, with the First Somerset Militia, the Royal Miners, a detachment of the 10th regiment of reserve, a squadron of the Royal Dragoon Guards, the Exeter Artillery, and the Artificer's Corps, attended by their field pieces, were brigaded on Haldon, where they were met by Lord Clifford's squadron of yeomanry cavalry, Lord Courtenay's regiment of volunteer infantry, the Chudleigh volunteers, and the light company of the Second Somerset. The business commenced by an attack on a strong position, at the entrance of Haldon, on the Newton Road, which was difficult of access, and strengthened by artillery; the light*

troops having, however, driven in the advanced posts, and the sharp-shooters sent out to annoy them, the artillery, etc. retreated towards the race stands, where they were vigorously pursued by the attacking army. The firing was kept up on each side with great vivacity, and different positions were taken to show the manner of forming, in case of actual service.

Although not invaded, Devon was very much at war. Its troops and sailors played a major role in the successive wars with France. The impact of war was varied. One of its most lasting consequences is still seen on Dartmoor at Princetown. Sir Thomas Tyrwhitt, Lord Warden of the Stannaries, decided to build large barracks for French prisoners of war who, hitherto, had been largely held in `hulks', prison ships. These barracks, began in 1806 and opened in 1809, were to be the basis for Dartmoor prison. They were built in accordance with the customary radial pattern that was seen as the most progressive, not least because it made surveillance easier. Five blocks were originally planned, but another two were added in 1812. The prison, which, at the close of 1812, housed 9,500 prisoners and a garrison of 1,200, was the basis of a new small town, including a church, St Michael, of 1813, a period in which church building was limited.

Tyrwhitt saw his prison as part of a system to develop Dartmoor. The prisoners were to act as a labour force. He was responsible for the Plymouth and Dartmoor railway which opened in 1823, while granite quarries were developed near Princetown.

Another consequence of war was greater difficulties for smugglers. The naval blockade of France was matched by the construction of a chain of naval signal stations on the English coast. Smuggling revived with the coming of peace, but in 1822 the Coast Guard was founded and this, eventually, led to a new coastal order with smugglers facing increasing difficulties; although changes in taxation policy, with the dropping of duties, were also important.

THE
TOWNS

Plymouth's naval functions led to the town becoming distinctly urban working class in character. The town spread considerably but not sufficiently to keep pace with the growth in population. As with other large urban areas there was a decline in quality of life, in particular as a result of overcrowding. Multiple-occupancy was combined with indifferently built houses, and the net result, as elsewhere, was unsanitary housing conditions. The cholera that hit Plymouth hard in 1832 was one comment on Georgian Devon. Plymouth's growth provided employment for those seeking work across Devon. It also served to draw in labour from further afield. Thus, some skilled Welsh migrants moved to the city.

Town life was very different to that in rural areas, as townspeople were exposed to many other individuals on a daily basis, and this contributed to the fluidity of society there. Nevertheless, there was a consistent framework in both town and country. Social relationships and attitudes reflected a clear cultural inheritance and the prevalent economic and technological environment. The Judaeo-Christian inheritance, clearly enunciated in the laws and teachings of the churches, decreed monogamy, prohibited marriage between close kin, stipulated procreation as a purpose of matrimony while condemning it outside, denounced abortion, infanticide, homosexuality and bestiality, made divorce very difficult, enforced care of children, venerated age, and ordered respect for authority, religious and secular, legal and law-enforcing. Other issues that would be more regulated today, such as spousal abuse and rape within marriage, were ignored. Economic productivity was low, there was little substitute for manual labour, and the value accrued through most labour was limited. Most of the population neither controlled nor produced much wealth, and the principal means of acquisition was by inheritance. The dominant ethos was patriarchal, hierarchical, conservative, religious and male-dominated, although each involved both tensions and a variety of expressions.

The economy of the poor was such that employment was the essential condition for most women. The arduous nature of most of the work, and the implications of family and social life, together defined the existence of the majority of women.

The use of the household as the basis for social organisation led to an emphasis on the role of men, because they were regarded as heads when they were present. The legal rights of women were limited, not least their rights to own and dispose of property. Yet, it would be mistaken to minimise the role of women. The major shift from women-only midwifery to a situation by the 1770s in which increasing numbers of children were being delivered by male midwives reflected the choices of mothers, not the imposition of male structures of control.

Women were of great importance as consumers. The extent to which the individual family lived together in close proximity led to a need for cooperation and mutual tolerance that necessarily affected the authority of husbands and fathers. In addition, the inoculation of deference, discipline and piety by authoritarian parents was not incompatible with affection.

The idea of equality between men and woman was increasingly approved of, but the general notion of equality was one of respect for separate functions and development.

Exeter had become a centre for the `middling' sort, largely professionals and gentlemen merchants. Service activities were fostered by the improvement of communications in the county and became more significant than the town's industrial role. The growth in urban functions ranged widely. The Devon & Exeter Hospital opened in 1743, the first banks in the city opened, the Exeter Bank in 1769 and the Devonshire Bank in 1770, the Law Courts were built in 1773-5, the first gasworks for Exeter were established on Bonhay in 1817 and the Grecian Baths in 1821. The changing urban fabric included the removal of the four city gates from 1769 to 1819, the building of Bedford Crescent from 1773, and the building of brick crescents – Barnfield in 1792 and Colleton from 1802. Brick buildings with large windows were built in a regular `classical' style along new streets. In Plymouth, Durnford Street and Emma Place were laid out in 1773 as a fashionable residential area. Paving was extended to existing thoroughfares in Tiverton under an Act of 1794.

Timber and thatch were seen as dated, unattractive, non-utilitarian and, increasingly, non-urban. Alongside light, roomy and attractive private houses for the affluent, public and philanthropic buildings were built across the county. This was linked to the development of resorts and service functions, and to a shift in the urban hierarchy, with the cloth industry becoming less important. Circulating libraries and theatres were opened including, for the former, at Sidmouth, Dawlish, Exmouth and Teignmouth by 1815, and, for the latter including, although with only limited lasting success, in Sidmouth, Exmouth and Teignmouth.

Demand for goods interacted with the development of shops. This transformed townscapes. Shops complemented, and competed with, markets, and also with other settings for trades, such as private dealings in inns, and peddlers and chapmen. This was part of the process by which towns were increasingly differentiated from what were to become villages. The transformed townscape included the removal of markets from town streets to purposely built market house, as in Tiverton in 1830 and Crediton in 1836. Honiton High Street lost its shambles in 1823.

The development in service functions was also seen with the growth of resorts along the south coast, for example Sidmouth. Fortfield Terrace, Sidmouth, was begun in 1792, and there were also efforts to provide genteel housing in Exmouth and Torbay in the 1790s. Assembly rooms opened in Exmouth in 1801, Dawlish following in 1811. Den Crescent at Teignmouth followed in 1826. This coast became a fashionable place to live and retire, and this helped lead to a distinctive social and demographic structure. In contrast, the north Devon coast was less fashionable, although it attracted trippers from South Wales. The gentility, politeness and refinement conspicuously displayed in the South Devon resort towns, with their approximations of Bath society, were absent there.

As yet, the interior of the county attracted few tourists. There was a developing cult of `Romantic' landscapes in Britain, but that focused on the Lake and Peak Districts and the Wye Valley rather than Dartmoor or Exmoor, although aesthetic interest in the Devon countryside increased towards the end of the period. Viewpoints such as Haldon Hill attracted visitors. Improving landowners saw what they referred to as `waste' as a challenge. Thus Denys Rolle (1725-97), who disliked Dartmoor and Exmoor, was keen on enclosure and soil improvement by manuring, and sought to cultivate Woodbury Common. Rolle, MP for Barnstaple from 1761 to 1774, was a prominent colonial entrepreneur, seeking to develop first East Florida and then the Bahamas.

POLITICS

Aside from the two MPs from the county seat, a number of Devon towns were parliamentary boroughs, again each with two MPs: Ashburton, Barnstaple, Bere Alston, Dartmouth, Exeter, Honiton, Okehampton, Plymouth, Plympton, Tavistock, Tiverton and Totnes. Devon's 26 MPs made up a high percentage of the 558 MPs in Parliament after the Union of England and Scotland in 1707. The franchise and

size of the electorate in Devon
constituencies varied: in the early
eighteenth century, from 2,099 voters
exercising the vote in the county
constituency of Devon in 1712, and about
1,500 in Exeter, where the franchise
rested with the freeholders and freemen,
to 18 to 30 in Bere Alston, where only the
holders of burgage properties could vote,
and 24 in Tiverton, where only the
corporation could vote.

The nature of the political world
varied greatly. On 25 August 1724, Robert
Walpole, the leading minister, visited
Exeter with his heir, Robert, as well as
George Dodington, William Yonge, MP
for Honiton, Richard Edgcumbe, MP for
Plympton Erle, and Charles Churchill,
dining at the bishop's palace and being
presented with the freedom of the city, a
sign of his popularity and presence

reported in the press. This was the politics of patronage at its most prominent. Walpole also had Stephen Weston, one of his former teachers at Eton, made Bishop of Exeter. With this he held the rectory of Shobrooke, the treasureship of Exeter Cathedral, and, finally, the archdeaconry of Exeter. His son Stephen became Registrar of the diocese and the latter's son Stephen was also a Devon cleric.

The emphasis in scholarship on the period has lately been on the rise of a `public' political world. Stress has been placed on the development of newspapers. Exeter, where the first press was founded in 1678, early on had not only one but two newspapers putting it on the top level of provincial newspaper centres. The total circulation of the *Exeter Gazette* in 1713 was about 1,000. Elsewhere in Devon, however, the press developed far more slowly.

Newspapers established in Plymouth in 1718, 1758 and 1780 all failed after a few years, although in 1808 two rival newspapers were founded there and continuous newspaper production in the town began. However, the first newspaper in North Devon, the Barnstaple-based *North Devon Journal*, was not founded until 1824, and the first in South Devon, at Torquay, not until 1839. Tavistock and Teignmouth did not get their own papers until 1847.

The press had been keen to satisfy political interests, if not to develop political consciousness. The *Exeter Gazette or Universal Advertiser for the West of England* of 26 December 1793 declared that its goal was to give `our readers the earliest statement of political events, as well as to supply them with every entertainment a weekly register of occurrences would permit'. A more activist tone was set in the early nineteenth century. *The Devonshire Chronicle and Exeter News*, a keen supporter of parliamentary reform, sought to stir up a local response in its issue of 9 July 1831 by printing a list of how Devon, Cornwall and Somerset MPs had voted on the second reading of the Reform Bill.

Such an approach to the politics of the period, however, would be misleading. Devon was not a hotbed of radicalism. Indeed, in November 1792, John Hatsell, Clerk to the House of Commons, wrote:

> *I wish every county was like Devonshire – but I fear that in Ireland, Scotland, the manufacturing parts of Yorkshire and particularly in London, there is a very different spirit rising.*

The county parliamentary seats were Tory strongholds. Uncontested elections between 1712 and 1790 (as before 1712) left successive Bampfyldes, Courtenays and

Rolles as MPs. Sir William Courtenay, the second baronet (1676-1735) of Powderham Castle, was MP for the county from 1701 to his death. Uncontested elections kept down the cost of politics and accorded with the widely-held expectation that hierarchy and consensus should be maintained. There was pressure for representation to be balanced between the western and eastern districts, but the tensions, which led to a disputed election in 1712, were between High and Moderate Tories. In 1711, John Oldmixon wrote that `Devon has preserved its pinnacle principles very punctually'. Tory dominance of the county led the Whig gentry to focus their efforts on the borough seats, ensuring that they became the centre of political contention. The Courtenays were also Lords of the manor of Honiton, where they appointed the Returning Officer as well as other officials. Sir

William's oldest surviving son, William, sat for Honiton from 1734 until 1742 when he was elected for Devon which he sat for until 1762 when he was made Viscount Courtenay. His brother Henry sat for Honiton from 1741 until 1747 and from 1754 until his death in 1763. The paternalistic character of politics was captured by the elder Sir William, who, in 1733, told the House of Commons that Honiton was against the Whig government's Excise scheme:

> He knew the borough... he knew almost every man in it, he had but lately come from there, and he knew that they were all against it. The whole people of that country were against it and had joined in their salutations for him to come up of purpose to it.

The other Honiton MP from 1715 until 1754 was William Yonge of Colyton, a Whig.

The Yonges held the estate of Batishorn near Honiton and were influential in the town. However much parliamentary seats were under the influence of patrons, they still expected to be consulted and managed. This was true for example of the interest of the Duke of Bedford at Tavistock, of the Edgcumbes and Trebys at Plympton Erle, and of the Dukes of Bolton and Somerset at Totnes. Some boroughs saw shifting patterns of control. In Totnes, the elections of 1780 and 1784 were uncontested, as control over the two seats was divided between the Duke of Bolton and the Churston Ferrers interest deployed by Francis Buller. At Okehampton, patronage shifted, with Thomas Pitt of Boconnoc in Cornwall and the Duke of Bedford the dominant interests in mid-century, until Pitt's Okehampton estate was sold first to Lord Clive and then to Earl Spencer.

THE
ARISTOCRACY

Many of the aristocratic (and other) patrons had their seats outside Devon and this contributed to an important feature of the county's politics, society and culture. It was predominantly a gentry, not an aristocratic, county, and there were relatively few of the large country seats and extensive landscape gardens associated with William Kent, Lancelot `Capability' Brown, and others. Relatively few was not the same as none. Brown, for example, was active at

the Clifford seat at Ugbrooke. Robert Adam
had rebuilt the house for the 4th Lord
Clifford from 1763 to 1766. Aside from
work on the exterior, he extensively
redecorated the interior. The park, with its
two lakes, was given its present form by
Brown in the 1770s. His work was
celebrated in `A Poem on Ugbrooke' by
Father Joseph Reeve, a Clifford chaplain:

> *To shade the hill, to scoop and swell*
>   *the green,*
> *To break with wild diversities the scene*
> *To model with the Genius of the place*
> *Each artless feature, each spontaneous*
>   *grace.*

At Powderham, James Wyatt added a large
neo-Gothic apsidal-ended music room for
the 3rd Viscount in 1794-6. Earlier in the
century, a grand staircase was added in
1754-6 supported by exuberant Baroque
decoration. Other eighteenth-century

additions at Powderham included large Baroque bookcases dated 1740. At Saltram, the Parkers extensively rebuilt the Tudor house to produce a splendid exterior with excellent Adam interiors in which a number of Reynolds' paintings hang. The park was also developed in the style of Capability Brown by a Mr Richmond. George III visited Saltram in 1789.

However, the county's gentry character was important to its character. It also helped define the character of Exeter, as it served as the service centre for a large gentry world. Government interest was strong at Dartmouth and Plymouth, while in Exeter the Tory and High Church Corporation was the dominant interest, although it was challenged by those who opposed this dominance, the Whigs winning both seats in 1734. In 1776, backed by the Dissenters, and the mercantile interests, John Baring, a wealthy clothier and banker, who had founded the Devonshire Bank in Exeter, won a parliamentary contest going on to hold the seat until 1802. Corruption was of particular importance in Barnstaple elections.

RELIGION

Religious divisions were important in politics, although there was no close correspondence between religious and political alignments. The Tories, however, tended to be the Church of England party, while most Dissenters backed Whigs in the first half of the eighteenth century and radicals thereafter. At least 113 Dissenting meeting-houses had been registered in Devon by 1701, while, in Exeter, two Dissenter meeting-houses were opened in about 1687 (and others by 1715 and 1760), followed by a Quaker meeting house in 1715, a Baptist church in 1725, an Independent chapel by 1744, and a synagogue in 1763. Plymouth's Ashkenazi Synagogue dates from 1762.

Methodism, initially an evangelist tendency within both the Church of England and the Dissenting movement, became more important in the second half of the century, especially in North and West Devon, although it was more prominent in Cornwall, where it proved particularly attractive among tinners and fishermen.

The response from the Established Church was initially hostile. There was a violent reaction to a Methodist meeting in Exeter in 1745, while George Lavington, Bishop of Exeter from 1747 until his death in 1762, in his *Enthusiasm of Methodists and Papists Compared* (in three parts, 1749-51) claimed that Methodism imitated the enthusiastic excesses of medieval Catholicism, with visions, exorcisms and healing; although John Wesley, in fact, argued against excessive emotionalism and enthusiasm. Lavington similarly published an attack on the heterodox Moravian Brethren in 1755.

However, Lavington's stance was not followed by all of the Established clergy. John Ross, a later bishop, was far more friendly to the Methodists. He invited Wesley to dinner, ignoring criticism that he did so, and Wesley was pleased by `the dinner, sufficient but not redundant, plain and good, but not delicate', and also with Ross's `genuine unaffected courtesy'. With time, the consolidation of the

Methodist position was entrenched with imposing churches, such as that built in Plymouth in 1813.

THE
EARLY
NINETEENTH
CENTURY

Devon's economy made a good recovery from the War of American Independence (1775-83), but the wars with France in 1793-1802, 1803-14 and 1815 had a more serious impact as they affected export markets as a whole. The woollen industry was badly hit. However, agriculture benefited from buoyant domestic demand, especially for the navy. In Devon, however, as elsewhere, there was a serious post-war (post-1815) recession that stemmed, in part, from demobilisation. Agriculture was hit, with grain prices falling, but the Corn Law passed in Parliament helped keep the price of grain higher than it would otherwise have been. This helped foster urban radicalism and demands for change, helping to lead to a volatile situation that was to culminate, in the early 1830s, in pressure for parliamentary reform. The problems of the rural economy hit the urban service-sector and Exeter experienced only limited growth in the 1820s.

The old order was very varied. From the 1830s, as reform became more self-conscious as a political cause, in both Church and State, there was a habit of denouncing `old corruption' and attacking the pre-Reform political system as corrupt and the pre-Reform

Government as incompetent. These charges, however, were inaccurate, and sprang from partisanship and a failure to understand the character, political culture, and achievements of pre-Reform England. Alongside complacent clerics there were others (the majority), who ministered energetically to their flocks. Most government functions were discharged satisfactorily, and there was only limited hostility to the political order. The Exeter-based *Western Luminary and Family Newspaper,* however, attacked `a spirit of insubordination and discontent' in its issue of 4 January 1831.

Many Devon readers would have agreed with this Tory and Church newspaper. Indeed, Henry Philpotts (1778-1869) who had been consecrated Bishop of Exeter two days earlier, voted against the Reform Bill and in October 1831 clashed in the House of Lords with the Whig Prime Minister, Earl Grey. Philpott's opposition to reform led to violence in Exeter, with his son using coastguards to garrison the episcopal palace against an attack by local radicals. This, however, was a crisis that was rapidly overcome.

There was no comparison with the unsuccessful conspiracy in the West Country that had formed part of the Jacobite plan for an insurrection in 1715. The shift in political culture away from violence had left a lasting impact. Other major changes included the significant rise of population, the development of Plymouth as a large naval base with a significant working class, and the growth of the seaside resorts. The combined impact was to ensure not only that Devon was a less rural and agrarian county, but also that the nature of urban activities had changed considerably. Industry had become less important, and Devon's relationship with national life was increasingly expressed through Plymouth's naval base and the seaside resorts.

FURTHER READING

The specialist literature can best be approached through the footnotes to the excellent *Historical Atlas of South-West England (Exeter, 1999)*, edited by Roger Kain and William Ravenhill, *The New Maritime History of Devon*, edited by Michael Duffy and others, volume one (Exeter, 1992), *John Travis's The Rise of the Devon Seaside Resorts*, 1750-1900 (Exeter, 1993) and the *Devon Historian*. Much of value can be found by reading newspapers from the period. For general work on the period, Jeremy Black, *Eighteenth-Century Britain*, 1688-1783 (Basingstoke, 2001) and *A History of the British Isles* (2nd edn, Basingstoke, 2003).

A 'Cartwheel' tuppence 1797
(by courtesy of Exeter Museums Service)

Also available in the Concise Histories of Devon Series

Roman Devon	Malcolm Todd
The Vikings and Devon	Derek Gore
Devon and the Civil War	Mark Stoyle
Cromwellian and Restoration Devon	Ivan Roots
Devon and the Second World War	Nick Smart

Also by **The Mint Press**

The Devon Engraved Series

Exeter Engraved: The Secular City (2000)

Exeter Engraved: The Cathedral, Churches, Chapels and Priories (2001)

Devon Country Houses and Gardens Engraved (2001)

Dartmoor Engraved (2001)

The Travellers' Tales Series

Exeter (2000)

East Devon (2000)

Cornwall (2000)